ideals®
COUNTRY

More Than 50 Years of Celebrating Life's Most Treasured Moments

Vol. 54, No. 3

"I only know that summer sang in me . . ."

—*Edna St. Vincent Millay*

IDEALS—Vol. 54, No. 3 May MCMXCVII IDEALS (ISSN 0019-137X) is published six times a year: January, March, May,
July, September, and November by IDEALS PUBLICATIONS INCORPORATED,
535 Metroplex Drive, Suite 250, Nashville, TN 37211.
Periodical postage paid at Nashville, Tennessee, and additional mailing offices.
Copyright © MCMXCVII by IDEALS PUBLICATIONS INCORPORATED.
POSTMASTER: Send address changes to Ideals, PO Box 305300, Nashville, TN 37230. All rights reserved.
Title IDEALS registered U.S. Patent Office.

SINGLE ISSUE—U.S. $5.95 USD; Higher in Canada
ONE-YEAR SUBSCRIPTION—U.S. $19.95 USD; Canada $36.00 CDN (incl. GST and shipping); Foreign $25.95 USD
TWO-YEAR SUBSCRIPTION—U.S. $35.95 USD; Canada $66.50 CDN (incl. GST and shipping); Foreign $47.95 USD

Printed and bound in USA by Quebecor Printing. Printed on Weyerhaeuser Husky.

The paper used in this publication meets the minimum requirements of
American National Standard for Information Sciences—
Permanence of Paper for Printed Library Materials, ANSI Z39.48-1984.

Subscribers may call customer service at 1-800-558-4343 to make address changes.
Unsolicited manuscripts will not be returned without a self-addressed, stamped envelope.

ISBN 0-8249-1143-1   GST 131903775

Cover Photo
POPPIES AND DELPHINIUM
Larry Lefever/Grant Heilman

Inside Front Cover
THE SAND GARDEN, BALLATERSON, ISLE OF MAN
Henry John Yeend King, artist, 1855–1924
Phillips Fine Art Auctioneers
Bridgeman Art Library, London
Superstock

Inside Back Cover
SUMMER FLOWERS
Carlton Alfred Smith, artist, 1853–1946
Christie's Images
Superstock

A Summer Wish

Christina Georgina Rossetti

Live all thy sweet life through,
   Sweet rose, dew sprent,
Drop down thine evening dew
To gather it anew
When day is bright:
   I fancy thou wast meant
Chiefly to give delight.

Sing in the silent sky,
   Glad soaring bird;
Sing out thy notes on high
To sunbeam straying by
Or passing cloud;
   Heedless if thou art heard
Sing thy full song aloud.

Oh, that it were with me
   As with the flower;
Blooming on its own tree
For butterfly and bee
Its summer morns;
   That I might bloom mine hour
A rose in spite of thorns.

Oh, that my work were done
   As birds' that soar
Rejoicing in the sun:
That when my time is run
And daylight too,
   I so might rest once more
Cool with refreshing dew.

PASTURE ROSE
Franconia, New Hampshire
William Johnson
Johnson's Photography

Summer Morning

Diane Siebert

The summer morning, cool and clean
    Beneath a sky of blue,
Arises dressed in shades of green
    Bejeweled by drops of dew.

Then warmed by sun and chased by time
    She disappears too soon,
Maturing, moving past her prime
    Into the afternoon.

If

Lydia Brinker

If I could be for just one day
    Exactly what I chose,
I'd be a lovely flower,
    Perhaps a budding rose.

If I could gaze for just one day
    At beauty where it lies,
I'd watch the sun set on the sea
    And in the morning rise.

If I could do for just one day
    Whatever I desired,
I'd sing with voice so sweet and pure
    All souls would be inspired.

If I could ask for just one gift,
    For this, dear Lord, I'd pray,
To be a loving child of God,
    Today and every day.

THAT MYSTIC BROOK

Philip Van Arsdale

I love to wander 'long the brook
And follow every bend and crook
And listen to its murmured tune
That sings of drowsy days of June.

Here one may watch the fish below
That dart so swiftly to and fro
And catch a turtle's sleepy wink
As trusty dog stops for a drink.

Shy wildwood flowers dot the ground,
And peace and quietude are found.
Enjoying summer's gentle breeze,
I walk beneath the stately trees.

I reach a gurgling waterfall
And hear the whippoorwill's lone call
Then pass the boys' "old swimmin' hole"
That met a need within a soul.

I like to keep our rendezvous
And greet its spirit there anew,
That mystic brook that wends its way
With outstretched arms to meet the bay.

Overleaf Photograph
CEDAR CREEK GRIST MILL
Near Woodland, Washington
Steve Terrill Photography

OPAL CREEK
Marion County, Oregon
Steve Terrill Photography

Woodland Walk

O. J. Robertson

It's nice that you would share your car;
    The village store is not too far.
I'd rather walk, if you don't mind.
    I hope you think me not unkind.

You see, when I walk to the store,
    I always take a long detour
Through woods where shade is dark and deep
    Along green paths where cool winds sweep.

I know a place where violets bloom;
    Perhaps I'll pick some for my room.
If I step carefully, I may
    See chipmunks scatter from their play.

I love to cross the wood's quiet stream;
    On both its banks frail fern fronds gleam.
In pools below a waterfall,
    Dark minnows dart and crayfish crawl.

The woods have treasures many more—
    I may forget the village store
And stay for hours with bird and tree;
    Why don't you come and roam with me?

WOODLAND TRAIL
Near Yellow Medicine River
Minneota, Minnesota
Bob Firth Photobank

A Green Cornfield

Christina Georgina Rossetti

The earth was green, the sky was blue:
I saw and heard one sunny morn
A skylark hang between the two,
A singing speck above the corn;

A stage below, in gay accord,
White butterflies danced on the wing,
And still the singing skylark soared
And silent sank and soared to sing.

The cornfield stretched a tender green
To right and left beside my walks;
I knew he had a nest unseen
Somewhere among the million stalks.

And as I paused to hear his song
While swift the sunny moments slid,
Perhaps his mate sat listening long,
And listened longer than I did.

SUNFLOWERS, ZINNIAS, AND CORN
Near New Lexington, Pennsylvania
Steve Terrill Photography

From My Garden Journal
by Deana Deck

SUNFLOWERS

On the wall above my desk is a painting of sunflowers my mother painted when I was a child; in it, a ceramic vase holds thirteen sunny, heavy-headed blooms. Perhaps the reason the painting is one of my favorite keepsakes is that I've always felt an affinity toward the sunflower. I cook with sunflower oil. I snack on sunflower seeds and feed them to the neighborhood birds and squirrels. And as for the national flower, I would happily replace the persnickety rose (a European immigrant!) with our native, joyful, carefree sunflower.

Sunflowers have been a favorite garden bloomer for more years than one might expect. Scientists discovered remains of the plant in the Mammoth Cave National Park area of Kentucky that date back to 1500 BC.

Sunflowers were most likely first cultivated in the United States by Native Americans, who used the sunflower extensively. Dried seeds were a popular snack among all tribes and were used to make sunflower seed meal, which

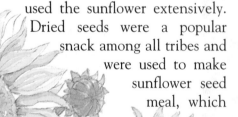

the Choctaws mixed with cornmeal to make tasty bread. The Iroquois used large quantities of sunflower oil, both to anoint the hair and as a base for pigments used to paint the skin for ceremonies. Other tribes used the different colors of shells and petals to make dyes for coloring fabric and baskets as well as for dyeing skin for rituals.

Early explorers to the New World carried sunflower seeds back to Europe, and the sunflower quickly became an important food and oil crop throughout Europe, especially in Russia. Today, it is still a major crop in Yugoslavia, Turkey, Romania, Argentina, and Africa. In the United States, sunflowers are commercially grown primarily as cattle and bird feed as well as for human consumption, but the flower's popularity in the garden continues to grow.

One reason for the sunflower's favorable reputation is its ease of cultivation. It enjoys full sun, requires no coddling, easily withstands droughts, and is not bothered by major disease or insect problems in a healthy garden. Seeds planted in the spring bloom in the late summer or early fall, adding a burst of color after much else has withered away. The seeds can be eaten, saved to plant again, or fed to the birds (they're great for attracting cardinals). To save yourself some work, just cut the heads when they're ripe and lay the entire flower near the birdfeeder.

Gardeners also love the fact that sunflowers can be grown in almost any condition. There are varieties that adapt to the wetlands as well as those which do best in desert-dry conditions. Some perennial varieties can even survive as far north as Canada. For those who prefer container gardening or who have limited garden space, dwarf varieties are the perfect solution.

Sunspot is one such variety; it produces twelve-inch blossoms on mere eighteen-inch stalks, blooms nine weeks after planting, and continues to bloom for up to six weeks.

To most people, the epitome of the sunflower is the huge, plate-size bloom atop a towering stalk. About the largest available is the Mammoth, which grows to a height of twelve feet and features flower heads a foot or more in diameter! But in truth, the large varieties are not very attractive in the garden, at least not for long. As soon as the flower finally opens that impossibly large blossom, it drops its head earthward. The reason is simple: survival of the species. The heavy head bends over so its seeds will fall to the ground instead of being devoured by hungry birds.

Birds are attracted to the largest blooms because they're easiest to spot. The result is that only plants with small blooms are overlooked by the birds and left to drop seeds to sprout in spring. Therefore, the sunflowers that are most apt to produce another generation in the wild are the plants that have the smallest blossoms. So it's no surprise that the wild sunflower is of the small-flowered variety. With its huge, gangly foliage, the wild sunflower looks better along roadsides than squeezed into a garden. A more domesticated version, the *Helianthus x laetiflorus*, has the same three-inch blooms as the native but with much more mannerly foliage. I've found this cheerful plant to be a great source of long-lasting cut flowers.

In addition to the variety of sizes available, a surprising variety of colors pleases sunflower enthusiasts nationwide. Garden catalogs tout sunflower varieties in a surprising range of colors, from the Orange Sun variety, with fully

The garden king returns with broad and golden gaze the sun's brave stare.

—Nora S. Unwin

double apricot-orange blooms on four-foot stalks, to Sunburst Mixed, a colorful, four-foot plant that produces eye-catching blooms in varied hues—deep crimson, lemon, bronze, and gold. A similar variety, Parks Velvet Tapestry, comes in colors from bright yellow to deep wine-red. Another unusual offering is Italian White, whose four-inch blooms range in color from ivory white to a creamy primrose. By browsing through a selection of garden catalogs, you are sure to find the perfect size and color sunflower to brighten your garden.

Contrary to myth and poets, sunflowers don't turn their faces toward the sun on its daily trip from east to west. The sunflower orients itself toward the east, which is the perfect direction for me to see the sunflowers in my garden through my kitchen window. The window forms a sort of frame around the many vibrantly colored sunflowers that I've planted side by side. This framed view reminds me of my mother's painting hanging above my desk and of our common love of this sunny flower.

Deana Deck tends to her flowers, plants, and vegetables at her home in Nashville, Tennessee, where her popular garden column is a regular feature in The Tennessean.

An Angel's Garden

Mary E. Overmyer Stokes

Whene'er I see a flower
That is hidden mid the rocks,
High on a mountain ledge,
Or in some lonely, lofty spot,
I wonder if the angels
There have planted seeds to grow
Where they can give them tender care
And only they will know
The sweetness of their perfume
As each flower opens wide
And lifts its face to God above
From off the mountainside.

Do angels sprinkle them with dew?
Has God put color there
To brighten up the rocky crags
And perfume all the air?
For only God in heaven
Or His angels dare to tread
Above the darkest canyons deep
To plant a flower bed.

WATERFALLS AND ROCK GARDENS
Cypress Gardens, Florida
William Johnson
Johnson's Photography

Country CHRONICLE

Lansing Christman

SUMMER EVENINGS ON THE VERANDAH

There is something special about soft summer evenings in the country. The choicest part of the day may well be the long, placid evening in the tranquility of the hills. As the sun lowers in the western skies, it is a time of peace and reflection, a time for meditation.

Long years ago, most of the old country homes had large, vine-sheltered porches where families gathered after the supper hour. Men and boys found relief from a hot day's work in the simmering fields. Women and girls found the same comfort and ease, leaving the kitchen and its sweltering stove for the verandah with its latticed columns and climbing vines, the virgins-bower, or the wild clematis. I sometimes feel those evenings in the early years of the century played a major role in bringing families together and keeping them close.

During those evenings of days long past, there was a heavenly atmosphere that filled the soft hours of twilight: the coolness of the breeze, the fading calls and chirping of birds— the wood thrush and the robin, frogs thumping in the swamps and marshes, the tremolo of the crickets, the blinking light of fireflies, the aroma of the clovers and the wild evening primrose. Sometimes a Model T with its chugging motor would stir up the dust in the dirt road that passed the house. We did not mind. We were at peace.

On those rural evenings seventy years ago, I loved to sit under the shelter of the verandah and look out at the meadow where haycocks painted a bucolic picture across the field. The lowering sun spread across the newly mown meadow and created a charming country scene of elegance and beauty.

I still cherish day's end when the wick of the sun is turned low to reveal the moon and the glittering stars so high above. May we never overlook the glory and peace of summer evenings in the country.

The author of two published books, Lansing Christman has been contributing to Ideals *for more than twenty years. Mr. Christman has also been published in several American, foreign, and braille anthologies. He lives in rural South Carolina.*

EARLY SUMMER EVENING
Ludington, Michigan
Darryl R. Beers Photography

THE OLD PITCHER PUMP AND THE MULBERRY TREE

While tossing from fever, in dreams I can see
An old pitcher pump and a mulberry tree.
I hear songbirds singing in choir overhead
In praise of the berries of purple and red.
Provision for the birds and the bees God has made
With an old pitcher pump dripping under its shade.
The great spreading branches sway near to the ground,
And I feel the pump handle as I pull up and down.
I can taste the cool water, feel mud on my feet,
And smell the ripe berries so cloyingly sweet.
My light summer dress has once been a feedsack,
And heavy gold braids hang like ropes down my back.
Berry-brown hands lift the pail to my lips,
And I drink of its nectar in slow, thirsty sips.
They offer me ice cream and hot tea and toast,
But never the water that I crave the most.
So, when I am well I shall drive once again
In my little red car down a quaint country lane.
I'll watch for a farmhouse and someday I'll see
An old pitcher pump and a mulberry tree.

Ruth Roberts Douglas
Williston, Florida

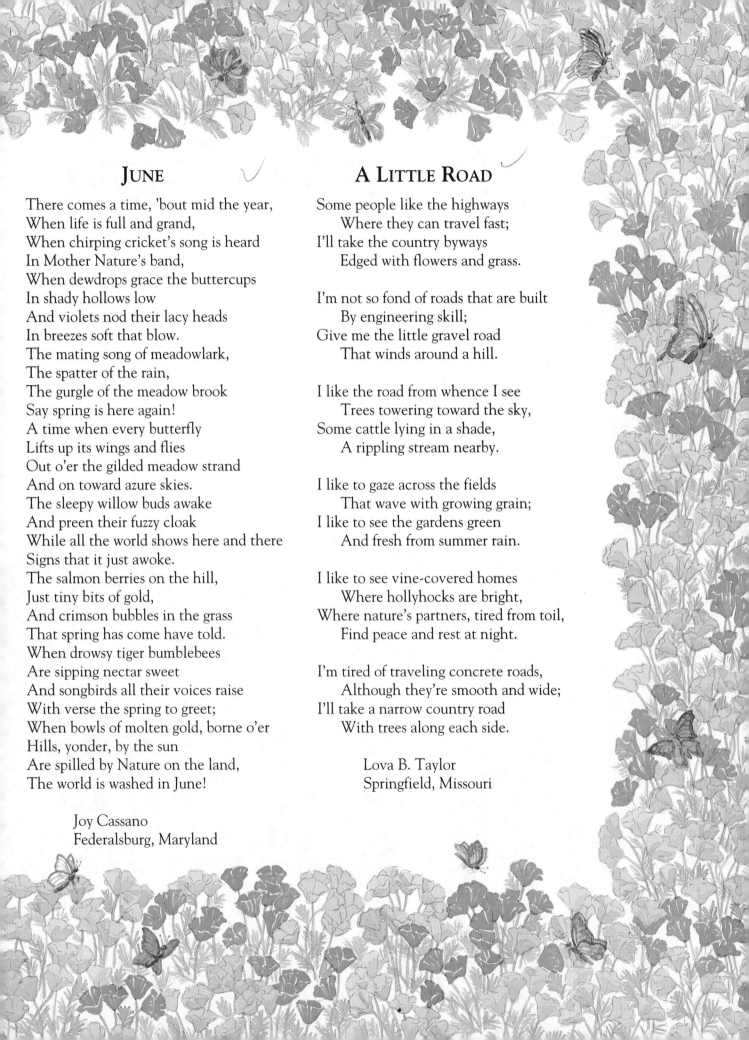

JUNE

There comes a time, 'bout mid the year,
When life is full and grand,
When chirping cricket's song is heard
In Mother Nature's band,
When dewdrops grace the buttercups
In shady hollows low
And violets nod their lacy heads
In breezes soft that blow.
The mating song of meadowlark,
The spatter of the rain,
The gurgle of the meadow brook
Say spring is here again!
A time when every butterfly
Lifts up its wings and flies
Out o'er the gilded meadow strand
And on toward azure skies.
The sleepy willow buds awake
And preen their fuzzy cloak
While all the world shows here and there
Signs that it just awoke.
The salmon berries on the hill,
Just tiny bits of gold,
And crimson bubbles in the grass
That spring has come have told.
When drowsy tiger bumblebees
Are sipping nectar sweet
And songbirds all their voices raise
With verse the spring to greet;
When bowls of molten gold, borne o'er
Hills, yonder, by the sun
Are spilled by Nature on the land,
The world is washed in June!

Joy Cassano
Federalsburg, Maryland

A LITTLE ROAD

Some people like the highways
    Where they can travel fast;
I'll take the country byways
    Edged with flowers and grass.

I'm not so fond of roads that are built
    By engineering skill;
Give me the little gravel road
    That winds around a hill.

I like the road from whence I see
    Trees towering toward the sky,
Some cattle lying in a shade,
    A rippling stream nearby.

I like to gaze across the fields
    That wave with growing grain;
I like to see the gardens green
    And fresh from summer rain.

I like to see vine-covered homes
    Where hollyhocks are bright,
Where nature's partners, tired from toil,
    Find peace and rest at night.

I'm tired of traveling concrete roads,
    Although they're smooth and wide;
I'll take a narrow country road
    With trees along each side.

Lova B. Taylor
Springfield, Missouri

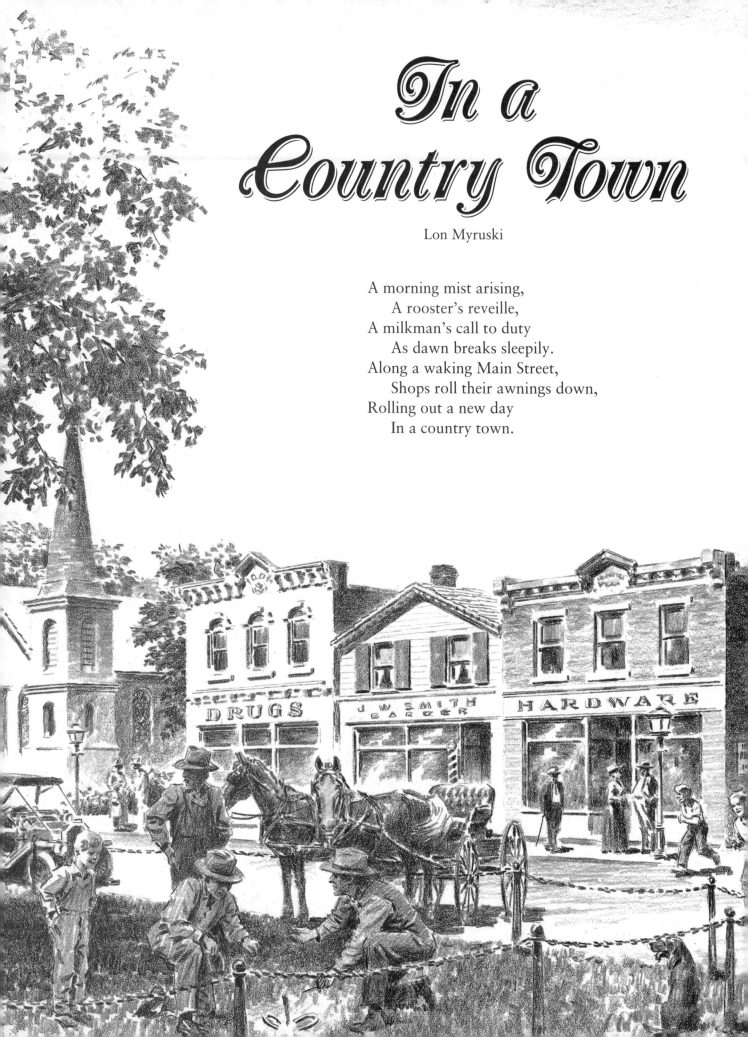

In a Country Town

Lon Myruski

A morning mist arising,
    A rooster's reveille,
A milkman's call to duty
    As dawn breaks sleepily.
Along a waking Main Street,
    Shops roll their awnings down,
Rolling out a new day
    In a country town.

A new-mown hay aroma,
    From fields yet to be gleaned,
Wafts in to woo the roses
    In bloom upon the green.
And there a game of checkers,
    With cheers as kings are crowned—
For life holds simple pleasures
    In a country town.

At midday on a corner,
    Lads sell their lemonade
As June bugs, larks, and bluebirds
    All render serenade.

It's so serenely rustic,
    The sweetness of the sound
Of nature's country music
    In a country town.

A day has reached an ending
    In this tranquil domain
As lightning bugs go dancing
    Amidst a gentle rain.
There's happiness in dwelling
    On what seems hallowed ground,
A little short of heaven
    In a country town.

Yesterday

Frances Bell Pond

I passed the place where I was born,
'Twas off the beaten track,
And felt a joy akin to pain
As memories flooded back.

The old farmhouse looked different now,
Yet somehow I could see
There standing by the kitchen door
My mother wave to me.

I followed Dad behind the plow
And walked the furrow straight
Then chased the cows up from the field
And rode the old barn gate.

Then in the dusky twilight,
When the shadows had grown long,
Across the tranquil pasture
Came a killdeer's plaintive song.

I smelled again the new-mown hay,
Mysterious, sweet incense,
And gathered gobs of daisies
Growing by the old rail fence.

My dog and I romped in the lea
'Neath sunshine warm and bright
Then drifted off to dreamland
In a featherbed at night.

I thank you, God, for yesterdays
So filled with warmth and charm,
For parents dear who loved me
On our cherished country farm.

MOUNT PHILO STATE PARK
Vermont
William Johnson
Johnson's Photography

Ideals' Family Recipes

Favorite Recipes from the Ideals Family of Readers

Editor's Note: Please send us your best-loved recipes! Mail a typed copy of the recipe along with your name, address, and phone number to Ideals magazine, ATTN: Recipes, P.O. Box 305300, Nashville, Tennessee 37230. *We will pay $10 for each recipe used. Recipes cannot be returned.*

LIGHT AND LUSCIOUS STRAWBERRY CHEESECAKE

Preheat oven to 300° F. In a medium bowl, combine 1½ cups graham cracker crumbs with 3 tablespoons melted butter or margarine. Press mixture onto bottom and 2 inches up the side of a lightly greased, 9-inch springform pan; set aside. Separate 4 eggs, set aside. In a large bowl, beat one 15-ounce package part-skim ricotta cheese until smooth. Add ⅔ cup all-purpose flour, 4 egg yolks, 2 tablespoons grated lemon peel, 2 teaspoons vanilla, and ¾ cup granulated sugar; mix well. Stir in 1 cup nonfat sour cream and blend thoroughly. In a medium bowl, beat 4 egg whites until stiff but not dry; fold into cheese mixture. Pour into prepared crust; smooth top and bake 1 hour. Turn off oven and leave to cool 1 hour with door ajar. Cover and refrigerate until thoroughly chilled.

Purée 2 pints hulled strawberries; add ¼ cup granulated sugar and 4 teaspoons lemon juice; strain to remove seeds. Cover and chill. To serve, halve 1 pint strawberries and arrange over top of cake. In a small saucepan, melt ¼ cup red currant jelly. Brush top of cake with the melted jelly. Cut cake into wedges and serve with the puréed strawberries. Makes 14 servings.

Sheila Plowman
Vintondale, Pennsylvania

CHOCOLATE STRAWBERRY DELIGHT

Preheat oven to 450° F. Slice 5½ cups hulled strawberries. In a large bowl, gently stir together sliced strawberries and ¼ cup granulated sugar; set aside. In a large bowl, sift 1⅔ cups all-purpose flour, ½ cup granulated sugar, ⅓ cup cocoa, 1 tablespoon baking powder, and ¼ teaspoon salt. Using a pastry blender, cut in ½ cup unsalted butter until mixture resembles coarse crumbs. In a small bowl, combine ⅔ cup milk with 1 beaten egg; beat well with wire whisk. Add milk mixture all at once to flour mixture, stirring just until moistened. Spread dough into a greased, 8-inch round cake pan, building up edge slightly. Bake 15 to 18 minutes, or until toothpick inserted in center comes out clean; cool 10 minutes. Remove from pan; place on serving plate.

In a medium bowl, beat 1 cup cold whipping cream with 2 tablespoons powdered sugar until stiff peaks form. Arrange half of the sliced berries over cake; top with whipped cream. Garnish with whole strawberries and serve with remaining sliced berries. Makes 8 servings.

Cayce Terry
Franklin, Tennessee

ZELDA'S STRAWBERRY DESSERT

Preheat oven to 350° F. In a medium bowl, combine 1¼ cups sifted all-purpose flour with 2 tablespoons granulated sugar. Using a pastry blender, cut in ¾ cup butter or margarine until mixture resembles coarse crumbs. Press mixture into bottom of a 12⅜-by-8⅜-by-1⅛-inch baking pan. Bake 25 minutes; remove from oven and cool in pan on a wire rack.

Prepare one 3½-ounce package instant vanilla pudding according to package directions. Spread pudding over cooled crust; chill until set, about 1 hour. In a small bowl, mash 1 pint hulled strawberries; set aside. In a heavy saucepan, combine 3 tablespoons cornstarch and 1 cup granulated sugar; mix well and add mashed strawberries. Place over medium heat and stir constantly until mixture thickens and becomes translucent. Remove from heat; cool. Slice an additional 1 pint strawberries; stir into mashed berry mixture. Spread mixture over pudding in chilled crust. Spread one 8-ounce container non-dairy whipped topping over berry mixture. Makes 6 to 8 servings.

Mary Masten Kimmel
Surprise, Arizona

DELICIOUS STRAWBERRY GELATIN SALAD

In a small bowl, dissolve one 1-ounce package unflavored gelatin in ¼ cup cold water; set aside. In a medium bowl, dissolve two 3-ounce packages strawberry-flavored gelatin in 2 cups boiling water; stir in unflavored gelatin. Stir in one 10-ounce package frozen strawberries, thawed; 1 cup crushed pineapple, drained; ½ cup chopped pecans; and 3 ripe bananas, thinly sliced. Pour half of mixture into a large gelatin mold; chill until set, about fifteen minutes. Spread 2 cups sour cream on top of set mixture. Pour remaining gelatin mixture over sour cream. Refrigerate until set. Unmold onto a serving plate. Refrigerate unused portions. Makes 10 servings.

Rose Marie Carter
Conroe, Texas

A COUNTRY PANTRY

Helen Colwell Oakley

In my memories of long ago, most country houses had a pantry off the kitchen. The kitchens were large and roomy, but the pantries were small and compact, often no more than six feet wide by eight or ten feet in length. Grandma and Mom spent a great deal of time scurrying back and forth across our huge country kitchen as they prepared meals for the family—the sink was at one end of the room, the icebox at the other end, and the wood stove and kitchen cabinets quite a distance from the kitchen table, where food was usually prepared. But in the pantry, space was limited, with every inch used to advantage—few steps were required to prepare a batch of bread dough, churn the butter, or stir a pitcher of pancake batter. Cabinets with handy workspace on top surrounded the little room, and ingredients and utensils waited right at your fingertips.

A pantry was a mother's paradise. Luscious pies were rolled out, put together, baked in the wood stove in the kitchen, and then whisked back into the pantry to cool until suppertime; birthday cakes were magically decorated and stored away on pantry shelves for safekeeping, to be presented

Bread

later at a birthday celebration along with a freezer full of homemade ice cream that Mom had hidden away in the pantry beneath a layer of ice and several coverings of feed bags.

A country pantry was often the core of family life. The grandmothers, mothers, and daughters frosted cakes, mixed up cookies, and made biscuits and doughnuts as they talked with one another side by side in the pantry's tight quarters. Girls giggled and exchanged ideas and consoled one another as they nibbled on goodies from the bread box or perhaps freshly baked cupcakes or cookies from a tray. Little boys' and girls' hurts soon seemed much better after some tender loving care from Mom and a visit to the pantry for a special treat.

From time to time, the pantry became a kind of sanctuary where one could escape to find solace and renewed strength when life's burdens seemed too heavy to bear. In the beloved pantry, tears and sadness were soon replaced by hope and contentment in the presence of the past year's harvest: row upon row of quart and pint jars filled with shimmering preserves and jellies rested in the sparkling sunshine that streamed through the windows. Their beautiful colors gleamed like jewels. A full larder was a house well blessed.

In days gone by, the country pantry was the center of life and family. It held not only food for the body but also nourishment for the spirit. Perhaps someday my modern, rural home will be equipped with a pantry off the kitchen, just like those in my memories of long ago, when a pantry added country charm to my childhood home.

Vagrant

Isla Paschal Richardson

It was a recipe that I was looking for,
An appetizing salad or a quick dessert—
Somewhere I saw them in this magazine! I turn
The fascinating pages one by one . . . but soon
My vagrant eyes have wandered (as they ever do)
To find the little singing poems tucked away
Among the crowded pages. Truant eyes! I should
Have known I could not trust them for those recipes
With poems scattered through! And now it's time for lunch!
Surely that clock is wrong . . . I'll order cream and cake—
And while I set the table, lilting, shining words
Tiptoe across my heart—and I am singing too.
(Yet scolding editors who publish thoughtlessly
Those darling little poems near the recipes!)

Old Glory

Margaret Rorke

I'm just a bit of bunting dyed
In stripes of red and white.
My corner holds a field of blue
With stars to give it light.
Though winds may pull and tear at me
And sun my colors fade,
My spirit will remain as strong
As when I first was made.

My hist'ry is the hist'ry of
The land o'er which I fly.
Its freedom, pride, and power are
The things I signify.
I've been to all the battles that
My country's brave have fought.
I've dwelt in all the schoolrooms where
The youngsters have been taught.

I watch you stand as I go by
With hat upon your heart.
You see in me a nation great
Of which you are a part.
Unfurled and floating on the breeze
In red and white and blue,
Your faith in home and fellow men
Is passing in review.

THE FOURTH OF JULY, 1916
Frederick Childe Hassam, artist
Christie's Images, New York
Superstock

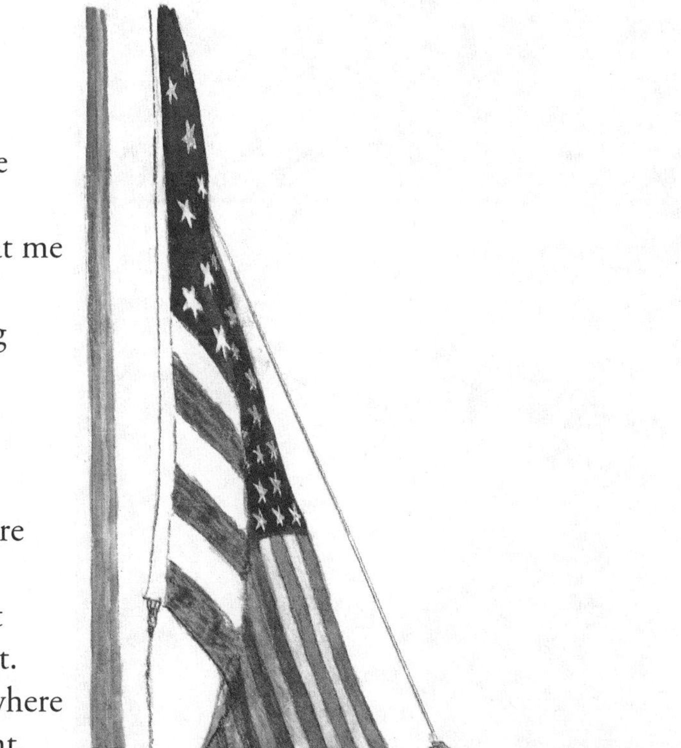

Lisa C. Ragan

Childe Hassam

Childe Hassam was truly an American painter. With a style that was uniquely his own, Hassam took his love for French Impressionism and applied it to distinctly American subjects, such as the cities of Boston and New York in particular. Although Hassam was initially criticized as being too "French" in his painting (he was often compared to Claude Monet),

over time the American public came to realize he was one of the legendary American artists. Through his individual style of painting and his images of everyday life in American cities, Childe Hassam embodied the ideal of the American Impressionist.

"I cannot remember when I did not have artists' materials."

—Childe Hassam

Born Frederick Childe Hassam on October 17, 1859, in Dorchester, Massachusetts, a suburb of Boston, Hassam's earliest artistic education began with his own creative play. As a young child of five or six, Hassam would carry his watercolor set to the family barn, climb into an antique coach, and paint "as long as a boy stays put anywhere," as he once said. As he continued to paint throughout his childhood, Hassam's Aunt Delia noticed his burgeoning talent and arranged for him to visit several local painters to supplement what little artistic instruction he received in the public school. All instruction ended, however, when his father's business was ruined in a fire and Hassam was forced to quit high school and find work.

After being fired from an accounting firm, Hassam turned to an occupation more befitting his talents and became the apprentice to a local wood engraver. In 1881, Hassam set up his first studio as a freelance illustrator. At first he divided his time between producing commissioned illustrations for magazines such as *Saint Nicholas, Harper's,* and *Scribner's* and doing his own private painting of watercolor scenes of the life around him in Boston.

Throughout the next several years, Hassam continued developing his skill with watercolors while receiving sporadic instruction through evening lectures at the Lowell Institute and study with artists in Boston such as the Italian painter Tommaso Juglaris. His first two solo exhibitions, which consisted entirely of watercolors, were held at the Williams & Everett Gallery in Boston in 1882 and 1884.

"There is nothing so interesting to me as people. I am never tired of observing them in everyday life.... Humanity in motion is a continual study to me."

Whereas Hassam studied briefly in Paris, traveling there in 1886 with his young bride, Kathleen Maude Doan, he considered his education there superfluous; his paintings from this period reveal a strengthening and refinement of the unique style Hassam had begun to develop in Boston. He was working more and more in oil painting at this point and found himself increasingly drawn to the everyday subjects of city life, an unusual theme for an Impressionist. Hassam sought to provide a glimpse of urban life that might be overlooked by the casual observer, such as horse-drawn cabs in Boston on a rainy afternoon or the effects of light and shadow on the New York City skyline.

Although he identified himself with the upper class (always procuring the finest accommodations that he could afford and wearing stylish clothes), Hassam nonetheless included a wide variety of social classes in his paintings; he could capture the beauty and dignity in both an affluent lady and an earthy shopkeeper. Hassam's thematic choices offered a revolutionary concept to the art world of the 1880s, which shunned modern subjects or settings. One critic even said of Hassam's work, "very pleasant, but not art." His oil paintings began to reap the praise of his peers and won him several awards, but he continued to receive little more than indifference from the American public. Hassam persevered, however, and always believed in himself and his art despite an initially cool reception from both critics and the general public.

"They are records if you will of America by an American."

Later in his career, Hassam achieved both commercial success and critical acclaim. By World War I he was at the height of his popularity. It was during this period that he painted his famous flag series, which depicted New York City's Fifth Avenue festooned in patriotic displays, with The Stars and Stripes as the most predominant. Hassam's patriotic fervor compelled him to paint twenty-four images in the flag series—an effort that was one of the greatest achievements of his career and of which Hassam himself was particularly proud. Not only was his subject matter again unusual for Impressionistic paintings, but Hassam also remained true to his unique insight into the typical life of an American city; in each scene of the flag series, the avenue below appears in its day-to-day aspect.

"I believe the man who will go down to posterity is the man who paints his own time and the scenes of everyday life around him."

Childe Hassam painted the everyday world around him—the cities in which he lived, the countryside he visited, the friends and family that filled his daily life. His wife Maude posed as his model in many images, although as his style became more and more abstract, it is difficult to discern her identity. The couple had no children and were apparently close companions who regarded their personal lives as very private. Hassam once said, "She is my business manager, legal adviser, and wife all in one." In the company of friends, Hassam loved a good argument but was also kindhearted and sometimes selfmocking. He counted among his lifelong friends fellow artists J. Alden Weir and John Twachtman as well as the poet Celia Thaxter.

A man of great physical strength and abundant energy, Hassam painted literally thousands of works in his lifetime. He continued to paint until just months before his death on August 27, 1935, at his home in East Hampton, New York.

Childe Hassam's paintings are now treasured American images that hang in museums across the country. More self-taught than not, Hassam was able to combine his artistic talent and love for America to render lasting records of his era. He stayed true to his artistic vision and painted his world in his way. And although the American public may have given him a less than warm welcome at first, Childe Hassam today can arguably be named the ideal American Impressionist.

A FATHER TO HIS FLAG

D. A. Hoover

"I pledge allegiance to the flag,"
I heard my father say,
And saw how proudly he beheld
Our colors on that day.

It was the "Fourth," firecrackers popped,
Bands played and clowns made noise,
A fun, exciting kind of day
For little girls and boys.
Then everybody was so still;
Old Glory marched on by.
I know I saw a tear of pride
Shine in my father's eye.
And then he smiled and said to me,
"My boy, of all you do,
Don't once forget this glorious sight,
Our own red, white, and blue!"

TRAVELER'S *Diary*

Ingrid Johnson

MOUNT RUSHMORE NATIONAL MEMORIAL
Black Hills National Forest, South Dakota

Until recently, I had never really thought much about Mount Rushmore. I knew that somewhere in South Dakota the heads of four great American leaders were carved on a mountaintop, and certainly I had seen countless photos of the stoic faces of Washington, Jefferson, Lincoln, and Theodore Roosevelt gazing with great dignity from a towering peak. But I had never really thought about what a grand thing it was that on a South Dakota mountain, more than six thousand feet above sea level, four spectacular works of art had been carved out of solid granite. I had never pondered what is, in fact, the impossibility of the sculptures of Mount Rushmore National Memorial.

But there I was, inside the Black Hills National Forest on a warm day in July, gazing upon the heads of Mount Rushmore bathed in the bright morning sunshine. Around me were the Black Hills of South Dakota, so named for the dense blue-black forests of ponderosa pine that cover their ancient slopes. In the distance, steep canyons and rugged peaks rose with great drama from the treeless plains all around.

The Black Hills are a spectacular place. It was easy to see why the great sculptor Gutzon Borglum, the man who gave the final sixteen years of his life to carving the heads on Mount Rushmore, chose this setting for his great work. The granite face of Mount Rushmore could not have presented a more perfect tableau: four hundred feet high with even-textured and fine-grained granite, and a three-hundred-foot, southeast face which looks toward the full day's sun year-round. And it was equally easy to

understand the great reverence that the Sioux have for this mountain and all the surrounding land; they gave these hills their name—*Paha Sapa*, hills of black—long before any sculptor laid eyes upon Mount Rushmore.

In the midst of this rugged natural beauty, Mount Rushmore stands out in brazen relief. It is humankind's handiwork on the face of God's. My earthbound imagination could not begin to comprehend the scope of the work, the task of carving these beautifully detailed heads on such a grand scale and at such a dizzying height.

But what moved me most at Mount Rushmore was the inspirational story of its sculptor. The son of immigrant parents and a child of the western frontier, Gutzon Borglum was a true patriot, and also a bold and boastful man. He laid eyes on Mount Rushmore in 1925 and declared to all who would listen that on its face he would carve the most spectacular monument the world had ever seen; for the remaining years of his life, Borglum devoted his every energy to fulfilling this boast. The patriotic sculptor envisioned his monument as a tribute to four great American heroes; but the work that emerged from the hard granite face of the mountain, the sculpture that draws thousands every year to South Dakota's Black Hills, is not only a tribute to Washington, Jefferson, Lincoln, and Roosevelt. Mount Rushmore is a monument to Borglum himself and to the land he loved. As I stood beneath the heads on Mount Rushmore on a sunny day in July, I gazed upon a tribute to the cherished American belief that all things are possible.

OUR HERITAGE

THE STAR-SPANGLED BANNER

Francis Scott Key

ABOUT THE AUTHOR

Francis Scott Key was born into a wealthy Maryland family on August 1, 1779. After a great deal of education, including St. John's College, Key decided to pursue a law degree. During the British attack on Washington, D.C., in 1814, one of Key's friends was captured. Key sailed out to the British ships to secure his friend's release and was detained at sea while the fleet attacked nearby Fort McHenry, Baltimore's only defense. During the long night of September 13, Key watched silently as the "bombs bursting in air" lit up the sky. When dawn broke, he was amazed to see the tattered American flag still flying above the bombarded fort and composed the words to "The Star-Spangled Banner" on a letter he found in his pocket. Francis Scott Key returned to his Georgetown law practice after the War of 1812 ended and was appointed, in 1833, the attorney for the District of Columbia, a position he held for the rest of his life. Key died on January 11, 1843; he was unaware that he had penned the words that, eighty-eight years after Key's death, Congress would declare the national anthem of the United States of America.

—Tara E. Lynn

O say, can you see, by the dawn's early light,
What so proudly we hail'd at the twilight's last gleaming?
Whose broad stripes and bright stars, thro' the perilous fight,
O'er the ramparts we watched, were so gallantly streaming?
And the rocket's red glare, the bombs bursting in air
Gave proof thro' the night that our flag was still there.
O say, does that star-spangled banner yet wave
O'er the land of the free and the home of the brave.

On the shore dimly seen thro' the mists of the deep,
Where the foe's haughty host in dread silence reposes,
What is that which the breeze, o'er the towering steep.
As it fitfully blows, half conceals, half discloses?
Now it catches the gleam of the morning's first beam,
In full glory reflected now shines in the stream.
'Tis the star-spangled banner O long may it wave
O'er the land of the free and the home of the brave.

And where is the band who so vauntingly swore,
'Mid the havoc of war and the battle's confusion.
A home and a country they'd leave us no more?
Their blood has wash'd out their foul footstep's pollution.
No refuge could save the hireling and slave
From the terror of flight or the gloom of the grave;
And the star-spangled banner in triumph doth wave
O'er the land of the free and the home of the brave.

O thus be it ever, when free men shall stand
Between their loved homes and the war's desolation;
Blest with vict'ry and peace, may the heav'n rescued land
Praise the Power that hath made and preserved us a nation!
Then conquer we must, when our cause it is just,
And this be our motto, "In God is our trust!"
And the star-spangled banner in triumph shall wave
O'er the land of the free and the home of the brave.

With Glad Voice Sing, America!

John C. Bonser

With glad voice sing, America,
　　Sing freedom's song anew;
The children of the earth still long
　　To hear that song from you!

Keep your resolve, America,
　　Make your great heart beat strong
As Pilgrims' hearts on Plymouth Rock
　　Bore all their hopes along!

Stretch forth your hands, America,
　　Those hands that shaped this land,
That they may help to mold a world
　　Where peace shall take command!

Stand firm on feet, America,
　　That will not cease to march
For noble cause and righteous laws
　　Beside a lady's torch!

Renew your faith, America,
　　One nation under God,
And plant the seeds of brotherhood
　　In freedom's fertile sod!

Lift up your eyes, America,
　　A dazzling vision see:
That day when people everywhere
　　Will share your liberty!

Yes, sing with pride, America,
　　Your song is welcome still;
From every hill its promise ring
　　And all our dreams fulfill!

CELEBRATING THE FOURTH
Linda Nelson Stocks, artist

©Linda Nelson Stocks

A Quaint, Old-Fashioned Home

Kay Hoffman

I like to see a modern home
In keeping with our time,
But none I find so charming
As the quaint, old-fashioned kind.

A home that has a lived-in look
With porch that's big and wide
Where hickory rockers, like old friends,
Are sitting side by side.

Where flowers bloom in time-worn crocks
To make each day more fair—
Not plants you need to pamper,
Just the simple garden fare.

A welcome mat placed at the door,
One of a home-spun style
With words of friendly greeting
Sure to bring the heart a smile.

Modern homes are nice to view
With their up-to-date design;
Still, it always warms my heart to see
The quaint, old-fashioned kind.

FAMILY ROOM CORNER
Jessie Walker Associates

BITS & PIECES

*C*an't you see the Creator of the universe, who understands every secret, every mystery . . . sitting patiently and listening to a four-year-old talk to Him? That's a beautiful image of a father.

—*James C. Dobson*

*T*he acid test of a father's leadership is not in the realm of his social skills, his public relations, his managerial abilities at the office, or how well he handles himself before the public. It is in the home.

—*Charles R. Swindoll*

*B*ecoming a father is easy enough, but being one can be rough.

—*Wilhelm Busch*

It is easier for a father to have children than for children to have a real father.
—*Pope John XXIII*

Fathering is a marathon, not a sprint.
—*Paul L. Lewis*

When I was a boy of fourteen, my father was so ignorant I could hardly stand to have the old man around. But when I got to be twenty-one, I was astonished at how much the old man had learned in seven years.
—*Mark Twain*

The father in praising the son extols himself.
—*Chinese Proverb*

One of the best legacies a father can leave his children is to love their mother.
—*C. Neil Strait*

Fathers' Prayer

Margaret Rorke

Dear Lord and Father of mankind,
    Forgive our foolish ways.
Give us the sight so we combined
Shall have the will to go and find
    Thy will this day of days.

Let every father 'mong us sip
    From faith forever true
And feel the strength that meets the lip—
The soul-felt sense of partnership
    In what he holds with You.

Today each looks with love and pride
    Upon his little clan.

Oh, let him know that glow inside—
That proof he is Your kind of guide—
    So precious to a man.

May those of us just starting out
    Remember homes we've had,
Resolving to make ours devout,
A tribute that will leave no doubt
    As to our kind of dad.

Help us to build with fam'ly flame
    Our heritage of clay
So it will bear no future blame
But lead lives worthy of Your name.
    This is our prayer today.

My Father's Hands

Bessie Saunders Spencer

My father's hands made dreams come true—
    A strong rope swing, a kite that flew.
I knew his hands by daily toil
    Would wring my living from the soil.
If I could feel his tender touch,
    No childhood sorrow mattered much.
Still on the album page we stand,
    I clutching tightly to his hand.

46

QUILTED WALL HANGING. Crafted by Mary Skarmeas. Jerry Koser Photography.

QUILTED WALL HANGING
Mary Skarmeas

Every Father's Day, I think back with a smile to the days when my children were young. Faces bursting with anticipation, they would thrust their crudely wrapped packages into my husband's hands for him to open. In earlier years, the gift was often a handmade coin tray or bookmark; but as they grew, the children pooled their allowance to buy their father a "real" Father's Day gift, which usually meant a tie. Many times, the tie was rather unusual, decorated with large animals or the children's favorite bright color. But my husband always raved about their perfect selection and wore the tie with pride to church the following Sunday.

Recently, memories of those holidays came flooding back when I came upon a delightful book by a woman who has discovered countless ways of turning men's ties into one-of-a-kind crafts. She was inspired by bags full of ties that she found in her father's garage after his death. Unwilling to part with them, she instead found a way to give them new life and, in the process, a way to preserve some of her warmest memories of her dearly loved father. I was moved by her story—and inspired to action. I could not bring back those days when my children were young, but quilting with ties seemed a wonderful way to remember those earlier times and create a craft rich in memories. At the same time I could use sewing skills learned by my mother, who taught me the value of using every scrap of fabric in quilting projects.

My husband had a good supply of discarded ties to get me started, and I asked my two sons for contributions as well. The wonderful truth is that all three of them were delighted by the idea that their old ties were of use to me, and they were eager to contribute to my quilt. After pouring through quilting books, I decided to use a traditional log-cabin design to make a simple, square wall-hanging quilt.

Log-cabin quilts feature strips of fabric interlocked to resemble the overlapping logs of a pioneer cabin. Some of the oldest log-cabin quilts even have small "chimneys" sewn on the squares to complete the effect. Traditionally, quilters chose a dark or warm-colored square for the center of each block to symbolize the cabin hearth, and the light and dark strips that surrounded the center square represented the firelight and the shadows cast from the hearth. The tiny pieces allowed the quiltmaker to make use of even the smallest scraps of fabric. Today, the traditional color scheme and design is varied to fit each quilter's tastes, but the charm and warmth of log-cabin quilts remain.

For a quilt such as the wall hanging I made, tie fabric makes up all of the "logs" or pieces, but additional fabric is needed for borders and backing. Look for the dressier fabrics—taffeta, moiré, silk, or brocade—in colors to complement your ties, and choose a good-quality lining fabric for your quilt. A book on quilting and a reliable pattern will provide all the details about fabric and other needed materials. A beginner might choose a simple wall hanging;

an accomplished quilter might create an heirloom bedcover. Regardless of the pattern and design you choose, however, what will make your quilt special are the color, texture, and character of the uniquely patterned ties. Before I started, I gathered my ties, spread them across the dining-room table, and then just spent time looking at them, rearranging them over and over again before I decided upon colors and combinations for the actual quilt.

The best way to prepare old ties for cutting and sewing is to undo all seams and remove the interfacing. After taking the ties apart, hand wash the fabric in cold water and line dry; then press with a warm iron. Since most ties are made from silk or another silk-like fabric, they have a tendency to slide during cutting, pinning, and sewing. To add body and stability, spray starch on the fabric's wrong side and then iron dry—this step will make the piecing of your quilt much easier.

Quilting books offer excellent instruction on how to piece and stitch your quilt. One of the easiest quilting patterns to construct, log-cabin designs usually require no quilting since the pieces are extremely narrow, are sewn on a backing, and have numerous seams. Their simple beauty and wide range of design variations make log-cabin quilts popular with expert stitchers and beginners alike.

As I was making my quilted wall hanging, it was fun to see the different personalities of my husband and sons reflected in the colors and patterns. Some ties I remembered specifically from a special occasion, others I recalled as gifts from Christmases, birthdays, or Father's Days. Other ties just made me laugh as I thought about how one of my boys still favors bright and loud patterns, much like those he selected as a child buying for his father. My finished quilt is both a lovely handcrafted heirloom and a tangible memory of past Father's Days when a simple tie represented hearts full of love.

Mary Skarmeas lives in Danvers, Massachusetts, and has recently earned her bachelor's degree in English at Suffolk University. Mother of four and grandmother of three, Mary loves all crafts, especially knitting.

AROUND THE WORLD WITH DAD

Reginald Holmes

I often sat upon his knee
 When I was just a lad
For nightly trips of make-believe
 Around the world with Dad.
We'd climb the Himalayas
 To hunt the bighorn sheep,
Or sail away to Africa
 And jungles dark and deep.
We'd visit ancient castles

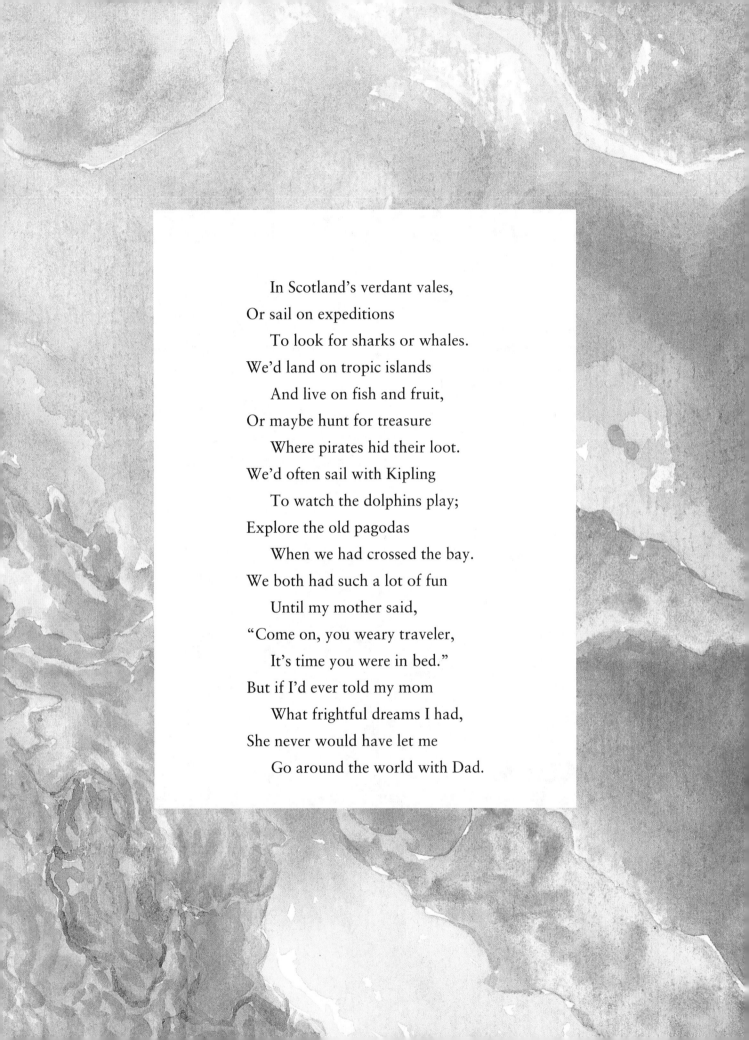

In Scotland's verdant vales,
Or sail on expeditions
    To look for sharks or whales.
We'd land on tropic islands
    And live on fish and fruit,
Or maybe hunt for treasure
    Where pirates hid their loot.
We'd often sail with Kipling
    To watch the dolphins play;
Explore the old pagodas
    When we had crossed the bay.
We both had such a lot of fun
    Until my mother said,
"Come on, you weary traveler,
    It's time you were in bed."
But if I'd ever told my mom
    What frightful dreams I had,
She never would have let me
    Go around the world with Dad.

A SLICE OF LIFE

Edgar A. Guest

A FATHER'S WISH

What do I want my boy to be?
    Oft is the question asked of me,
And oft I ask it of myself—
    What corner, niche, or post or shelf
In the great hall of life would I
    Select for him to occupy?

Statesman or writer, poet, sage,
    Or toiler for a weekly wage,
Artist or artisan? Oh, what
    Is to become of his future lot?
For him I do not dare to plan;
    I only hope he'll be a man.

I leave it free for him to choose
    The tools of life which he shall use,
Brush, pen, or chisel, lathe or wrench,
    The desk of commerce or the bench,
And pray that when he makes his choice
    In each day's task he shall rejoice.

I know somewhere there is a need
    For him to labor and succeed;
Somewhere, if he be clean and true,
    Loyal and honest through and through,
He shall be fit for any clan,
    And so I hope he'll be a man.

Edgar A. Guest began his illustrious career in 1895 at the age of fourteen when his work first appeared in the Detroit Free Press. *His column was syndicated in over three hundred newspapers, and he became known as "The Poet of the People."*

Patrick McRae is an artist who lives in the Milwaukee, Wisconsin, area. He has created nostalgic artwork for Ideals *for more than a decade, and his favorite models are his wife and three children.*

Grandfather Said

(To a Little Girl Who
Asks So Many Questions)

Marion Doyle

If I were old as the moon
And wiser than Solomon,
No doubt I could answer your questions—
To the last amazing one.
Then I could translate the rune
Of rain, and shadows spun
Of sunlight would no longer be
A baffling mystery to me.
I could tell how many flakes
In any winter's snows,
And why the leaf of aspen shakes
When no wind blows;
And why one says that daylight "breaks,"
And where a lost thing goes;
What lies beyond where the world's rim bends
And the very place where the rainbow ends.

Yes, the moon is so old; she knows
All the secrets of earth and heaven:
Why the petals differ on every rose,
Where the light of a burned-out candle goes.

If only I were as old as the moon,
Granddaughter of mine,
But I'm only seventy-nine!

Memories of Grandpa

Leigh Ross

I creep down the
Creaky stairs
And see my grandpa,
Bending over the workshop bench,
In a dim yellow lamplight,
His brown face etched with wrinkles
And firm concentration.
He rakes his fingers through
The sparse silver hair,
Carefully combed.

Then, looking up,
He spots me,
Walks over,
Scoops me up,
And sets me on the bench.
I watch him fiddle with the nails
And blocks of wood,
Munch on his homemade cookies,
Chocolate chip.
And I watch him
Skillfully carve the letters on
The delicate oaken box—
L-E-I-G-H.
I grin,
And Grandpa scoops me up
In a big bear hug.

A Welcome Visit

Cherri Franks-Turnbull

I hurried quickly down the road
In hopes I might find waiting there
Behind my lonesome mailbox door
A letter bringing words of care

From some loved relative or friend,
Who, distanced from me by the miles,
Would visit me through written word
To warm my heart and bring me smiles.

Sometimes on scented paper fine,
Adorned with blossoms, edged in gold,
Penned in the author's own sweet style
In ink which stood out dark and bold.

Received with no less joy, of course,
On yellowed sheets of tablet lined,
A childish scrawl across the page
I'd open up that door to find.

I'd read each sentence carefully;
I'd laugh aloud or shed a tear
To learn of how my loved one fared
And share the thoughts of one so dear.

Inside a pocket I would tuck
My prized possession safe away,
With each page ready to unfold
And read again throughout the day.

SWEETPEAS AT A COUNTRY ADDRESS
Near Alpine, Oregon
Dennis Frates/Oregon Scenics

Country Music

Anne Campbell

Country music holds a magic
    That awakens memory.
There are meadows in its phrases,
    And the farm enchantingly
Spreads itself upon our vision.
    We can see the small brown house
With the willow tree beside it
    And a child beneath its boughs.

We can see the old-time dances;
    We can hear the violins.
We are there to share the two-step
    When the evening fun begins.

We can hear our neighbor calling
    "Swing your partner! Do-si-do!"
And the tuneful country music
    That we heard long, long ago.

Only once in our long lifetime
    Have we found joy and release
From the trifling cares of childhood.
    In the country there was peace.
And we feel its tranquil presence
    And recall that old-time scene
When we glimpse through country music
    All the joys that once have been!

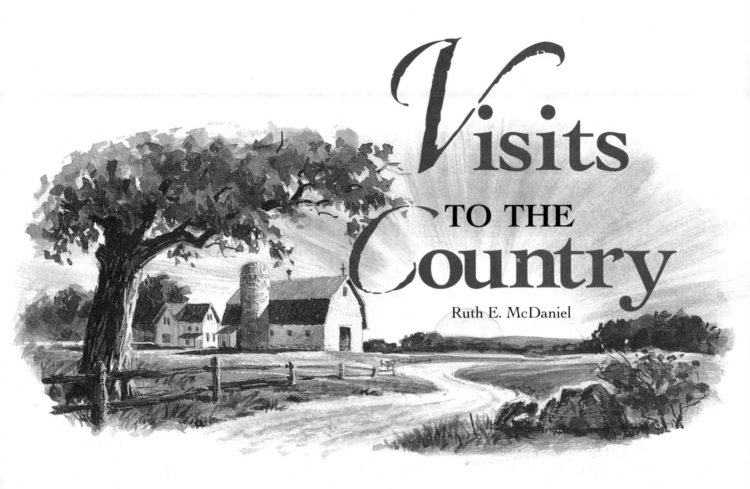

Visits TO THE Country

Ruth E. McDaniel

"Don't stop that boy!" Grandma would say
    In her direct, no-nonsense way.
"When he comes here, just let him be;
    A healthy youngster must run free!"

Grandma's philosophy was this:
    A hearty meal, a hug, a kiss.
Then turn him loose to splash in creeks;
    Let country sunshine tan his cheeks.

When we would drive out to her farm,
    The boys could play and do no harm.

Their balls could fly and hit no glass;
    They weren't told to "Keep off the grass!"

Our children, city born and bred,
    Ran wild and free, like Grandma said.
They loved the woods where they could roam
    And never wanted to go home.

And now they're grown, and Grandma's gone.
    But memories still linger on
Of country days spent, happily,
    At Grandma's, where life was carefree.

MATANUSKA VALLEY FARM
Below Chugach Mountains, Alaska
Jeff Gnass Photography

FOR THE CHILDREN

TREASURES
Mary Dixon Thayer

Down on the beach *when the tide is out*
    Beautiful things lie all about—
Rubies and *diamonds* and *shells* and *pearls,*
    Starfish, oysters, and *mermaids' curls;*

Slabs of black marble cut in the sand,
  Veined and smoothed and *polished by hand;*
And *whipped-up foam* that I think must be
  What mermen use for *cream in tea.*

These and a million **treasures I know**
    Strew the beach *when the tide is low*—
But *very few people* seem to care
    For such *gems scattered everywhere.*

Lots of these jewels I hide away
    In an old box *I found one day.*
And if a beggar asks me for bread,

    I will give him *diamonds instead.*

THE SENSES: HEARING
Jessie Wilcox Smith, artist
Fine Art Photographic Library Ltd.

THROUGH MY WINDOW

Pamela Kennedy

Art by Ron Adair

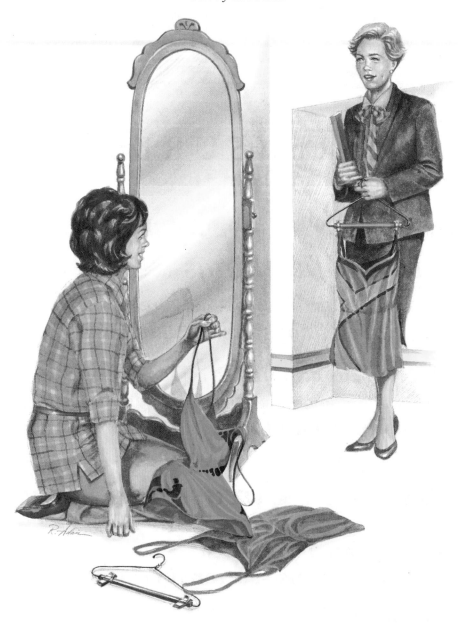

A SWIMSUIT SHOPPING SAGA

When Dickens wrote, "It was the best of times, it was the worst of times...," I'm sure he wasn't thinking about summer. But he never faced the dilemma confronting every woman when those lazy, hazy days roll around each year. For some it is the best of times when they pull out that slinky swimsuit and expose long, lean limbs for all to admire. For the rest of us, however, summer can be the worst of times as we try once more to find a swimsuit that somehow camouflages what autumn, winter, and spring have added to our figures.

This year I was determined to take the offensive. When the first swimsuit ads hit the paper, I was on my way to the mall. Surely in the preseason glut of swimming togs I could find just one suit that would be perfect.

I started looking at the two-piece numbers. Some of them weren't too bad, but others were perfectly horrible! I can't imagine anyone wearing something that is smaller than the price tag hanging from it! Even the more spacious two-piece suits left the obvious bare midriff—an expanse of winter white best kept under cover. That decided, I moved on to the one-piece suits.

At this juncture I was joined in my search by a helpful salesperson. "Marian, at your service" her nametag read.

"And what kind of swimming attire were you wanting this year?" she asked courteously, discreetly glancing at my hips.

I smoothed the front and sides of my tunic top. (I read in a magazine where longer lines are slenderizing.) "Well, something with a tailored look, not too skimpy, perhaps in a dark color (the same article said dark colors tend to minimize), maybe with vertical stripes." I stopped, realizing I was describing a zebra. I looked at her in despair. "I really don't know. What do you think would look good on me?"

She strolled around me, making little sighing noises, assessing the challenge before her. "Well, I'm sure we can find something that will do quite nicely."

I felt better already. "Quite nicely" exceeded my expectations. I had been willing to settle for "this will do."

My new friend Marian shepherded me to a dressing room and handed me several swimsuits to try on. I had no idea there were so many options. In short order we discarded the unstructured maillot and anything with French-cut leg holes, disproving the fashion adage "less is more." I vetoed a couple of styles Esther Williams would have been proud to wear. Some suits looked fine from the back, but not the front. Others were too busy or too glitzy or too frilly.

I was beginning to be discouraged when I spied a tag dangling from a yet untried suit. "Enjoy the figure Mother Nature forgot to give you!" it said. On the back of the tag was a diagram representing the inner workings of the "Wondersuit." It looked like an architectural drawing with arrows delineating "stress points" and "gentle pressure panels." This might just be the answer to my search. Excit-

edly I removed the "Wondersuit" from its hanger and, carefully following the directions, inched it on. I seriously suspected that if my hand slipped from one side of the suit while I was donning it, I could easily be propelled into the next dressing room as if from a slingshot! On the plus side, I felt smaller already. Cautiously I pulled the straps up over my shoulders and turned tentatively toward the mirror.

At that moment, Marian peeked in to see how I was doing. "Ooh, now that looks very nice! Very attractive. What do you think, dear?"

I nodded and smiled. For some reason I was having considerable trouble taking a deep breath. "Nice," I finally managed in a voice somewhat higher than normal.

She smiled and ducked back out of the dressing room. Actually, the suit did look pretty good. I had a waistline smaller than my bustline. Even my hips seemed acceptable, if not trim. And my posture was the best it had been since Mrs. Butler's poise class in high school. The suit was a bit snug, what with all the elastic inner workings, and I found it just a bit difficult to inhale; but on the other hand, there I was with the figure Mother Nature forgot to give me. What a dilemma.

Carefully I peeled off the "Wondersuit," took a deep breath, and got dressed again. As I emerged from the dressing room, I made a decision. Deep breathing is highly overrated. This year I plan to do lots of reading at the beach. I will go to the pool by myself so I won't need to engage in conversation. It will be a lovely summer of contemplation; certainly, the best of times! I handed over the "Wondersuit" at the cash register. "Marian," I confided with a satisfied grin, "*this* is the suit for me."

Pamela Kennedy is a freelance writer of short stories, articles, essays, and children's books. Wife of a naval officer and mother of three children, she has made her home on both U.S. coasts and currently resides in Honolulu, Hawaii. She draws her material from her own experiences and memories, adding highlights from her imagination to enhance the story.

REMINISCING

Karen Kuzminski

Night falls,
And the winds of time
Breeze through my mind
As I longingly find
Myself dreaming once more.

Of white beaches
And a blistering sun.
Of waves pounding
On the shore's apron.
Remembering nights
Of twinkling stars
When time seemed
Not to move so far.

Of picnics, parades,
And a summer escapade.
Of kite flying
One windswept day
Until entangled it became.
Climb, climb the tallest of trees
Fully prepared to free
This treasured creation.

And finding myself
Suddenly
Plunging to the ground
Amidst a field of wildflowers,
Their odorous aromas
Arousing my senses
Until I awaken to discover
The dawning of a new day.

CLIFF STEPS, MINSMERE CLIFFS, SUFFOLK (detail)
Charles Neal, artist
Superstock

The Little Things

Kay Hoffman

Lord, teach me to be thankful for
The little things in life,
The little joys we oft o'erlook
Amid the daily strife.

The first sweet rose in early June—
Face washed with morning dew,
The laughter of a little child
That warms the heart of you.

Lord, in the rush of daily chores
Bid me to pause awhile
To linger in the sunshine of
A neighbor's friendly smile.

And let me not be so involved
That I would fail to see
A robin teach her young to fly
And miss such ecstasy.

Sometimes a gift of joy is in
A little helpful deed
Or kindly word that someone offers
In our time of need.

Teach me, O Lord, to live each day
Above my meager self,
Ever thankful for the little things
More precious than all wealth.

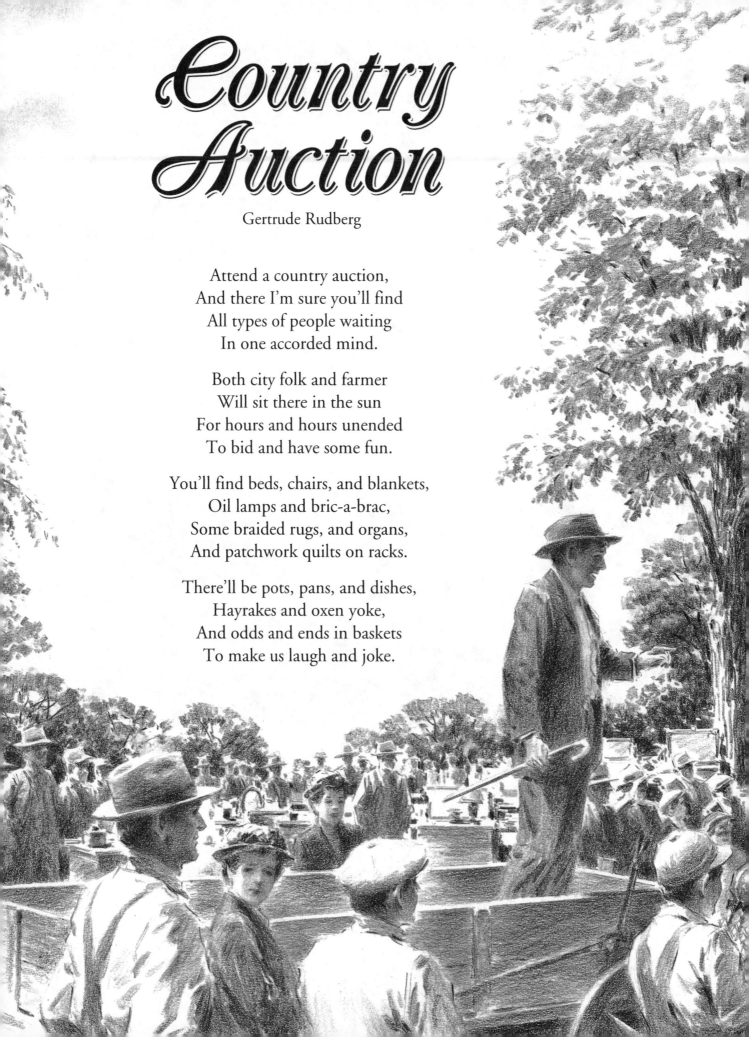

Country Auction

Gertrude Rudberg

Attend a country auction,
And there I'm sure you'll find
All types of people waiting
In one accorded mind.

Both city folk and farmer
Will sit there in the sun
For hours and hours unended
To bid and have some fun.

You'll find beds, chairs, and blankets,
Oil lamps and bric-a-brac,
Some braided rugs, and organs,
And patchwork quilts on racks.

There'll be pots, pans, and dishes,
Hayrakes and oxen yoke,
And odds and ends in baskets
To make us laugh and joke.

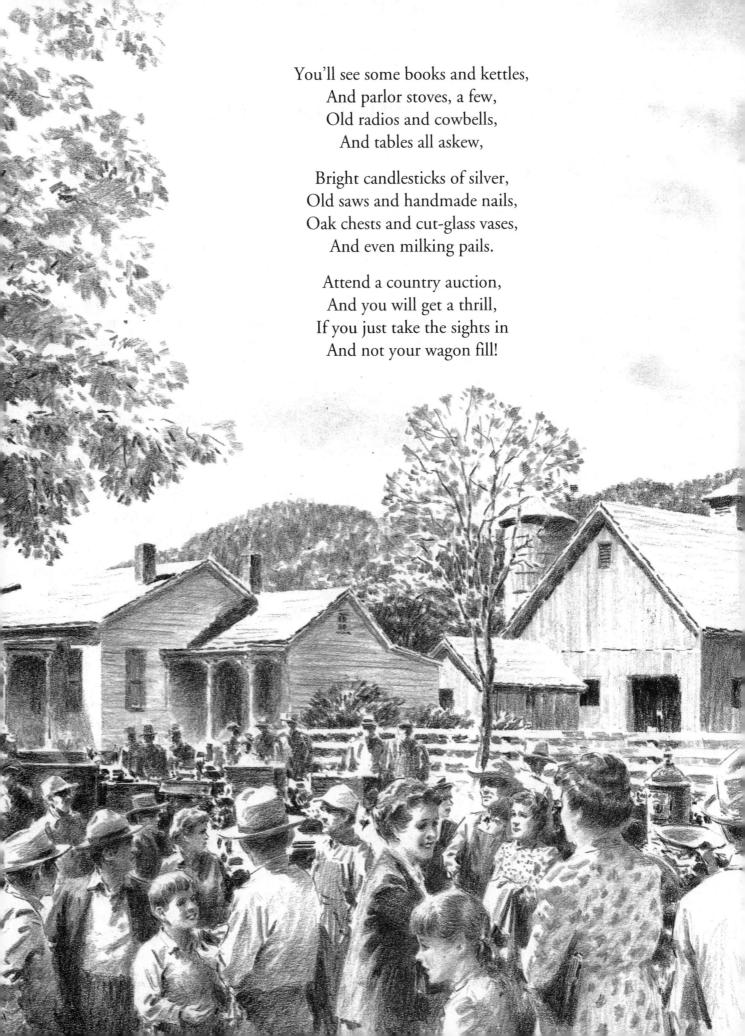

You'll see some books and kettles,
And parlor stoves, a few,
Old radios and cowbells,
And tables all askew,

Bright candlesticks of silver,
Old saws and handmade nails,
Oak chests and cut-glass vases,
And even milking pails.

Attend a country auction,
And you will get a thrill,
If you just take the sights in
And not your wagon fill!

COLLECTOR'S CORNER

MILK BOTTLES
by Melissa A. Chronister

On the windowsill above my kitchen sink stands an antique milk bottle filled with a bouquet of wild daisies. Once used by the Cloverleaf Dairy, the bottle is embossed with a large four-leaf clover; and the back is printed with the jingle "In the good old summertime, cloverleaf milk for me and mine." A reminder of times past, the bottle brings a smile to my face and takes me back to my childhood days in rural Missouri, when summertimes were carefree and farm-fresh milk appeared on the doorstep each morning.

I have always been drawn to memorabilia that recalls the charm and simplicity of rural life. So it's no surprise that several years ago, on a quick Saturday-morning jaunt to a local flea market, I purchased a particularly old-looking milk bottle made of amber glass. The intriguing bottle stirred my interest in learning more about the history of milk bottles. After some research, I was thrilled to discover that my dusty purchase was likely made in the early 1900s—a true find. I also learned that its dark amber color was intended to block the sun's harmful rays and prevent the milk from spoiling.

That amber bottle became the first in what is now my large collection of milk bottles. I have bottles of several colors now, including green, amethyst, and opaque white, along with clear glass. The differing colors were the result of a dairy's efforts to distinguish its bottles from those of other dairies. For similar reasons, dairies often labeled their bottles with a recognizable logo, title, or design, evident in five of my bottles that picture a cow and two with vertical stripes or "ribbons." Several others have large, raised lettering, which made it easier for carriers to identify each dairy's bottles in the pre-dawn darkness.

In all, my diverse collection contains several dozen bottles, representing dairies in twelve states—from West Coast Dairy to New England Farms. Most of my bottles are similarly shaped, yet several have flat sides or long necks. And although the majority of them are quart- and pint-sized bottles, I am especially fond of one tiny half-pint milk bottle, which was likely part of a child's school lunch in the early half of the century.

From a tin-topped glass jar to a large, unmarked gallon jug, my collection tells the history of the milk bottle's development. One bottle has the original cardboard cap which fit in its grooved neck, and another sports a swing-top, "lightning-seal" closure. I discovered perhaps my most innovative bottle at an antique mall. After a long, friendly chat with one of the shopkeepers, he offered me a discount on a bulbous-neck bottle from the Cream Top Company of Albany, New York. In good condition, the bottle even had its accompanying cream spoon, which was designed to hold milk below the bottle's bulge while the cream was poured off the top. The complete set was a rare discovery and a worthy addition to my collection.

In a way, I collected milk bottles even as a child, except then it was only by gathering my large family's empty bottles so that I could return them for the deposit. Now I prefer to keep the bottles I find, even those that boast of a hefty twenty-cent refund. As I continue to add to my collection, I hope to someday find a bottle from the dairy in my rural hometown. I can think of no better memento of my childhood in the country, where the summers were always long and the milk was always fresh.

DROPS OF INFORMATION

If you would like to start a collection of milk bottles, here are some interesting facts:

HISTORY

• A long-necked bottle that is dated 1866 and pictures a cow is believed to be the oldest glass milk container.

• In 1878, Brooklyn milkman Alexander Campbell was the first to deliver bottled milk instead of using a pail, can, or jar.

• Dr. Harvey D. Thatcher, a New York pharmacist and "father of the milk bottle," designed a "lightning-seal" closure in 1883 which consisted of a hinged metal stopper to resist spoilage.

• Most bottlers offered return deposits to encourage bottle return and reduce the bottlers' costs.

• The sides of many bottles were marked with the dairy's name; oftentimes, the bottoms were marked with the name of the manufacturer and patent information.

• From 1900–1940, disposable cardboard lids on glass bottles were the best technology available. Then, after cardboard containers were developed in the late 1940s, glass milk bottles were used less frequently.

• Prices on collectible milk bottles now range from a couple of dollars to over a hundred for rare specimens.

FOCUSING YOUR COLLECTION

Due to the wide variety of milk bottles, many collectors narrow their searches to one category. For example:

• Colored bottles, such as amber, green, amethyst, blue, or milk-white

• Bottles that have cardboard lid closures with specially designed grooves in their necks

• Milk bottles featuring cows, dairy farmers, birds, stars, or other embossed images or logos

• Lightning-seal bottles with hinged stoppers

• Glass baby bottles, which had attachable rubber tubes and nipples

• Sour cream, cottage cheese, or condensed milk bottles

ANTIQUE MILK BOTTLES. Ted Rose/Unicorn Stock Photos.

INTERESTING COLLECTIBLES

• Promotional milk bottles, such as miniatures measuring only two inches tall that were used for advertising in the 1950s

• Thatcher Milk Protector bottles, which in 1884 were the first milk bottles manufactured on a large scale and which were embossed with the image of a rural farmer milking a cow and the words, "Absolutely Pure Milk, The Milk Protector"

•Green milk bottles: the only known type ever produced was in 1929 for Alta Crest Farms in Spencer, Massachusetts; the bottles pictured a cow's head and the words "Mass-A-Seal, One Quart Liquid."

• "Babyface" milk bottles with bulbous necks shaped like a child's head

• Amethyst-colored bottles, which were originally clear but over time became discolored by the sun's rays

• Milk bottles bearing the name of your hometown: Walla Walla, Salem, Fairmount, Rochester, etc.

• Accessories to milk bottles, such as cardboard caps, cream separators, cap lifters, or metal racks for transporting bottles

The Traveling Circus

Elisabeth Weaver Winstead

The traveling circus with cumbersome loads
    Journeyed to town over long, bumpy roads.
The ringmaster shouts for the acts to begin;
    The jugglers keep bright-colored balls in a spin.

The tumblers bend backward and bounce up and flip,
    And skating brown bears glide with never a slip.

The seals clap their flippers and throw rubber balls
    While acrobats dive and swing up to the walls.

Ten rollicking elephants stroll, dance, and march
    As lions jump hoops in a big, golden arch.
Shot up through the air, human cannonballs burst;
    Then into the net they land safely, feet first.

The bareback queen stops her white horse on command;
    She bends and she swings in a graceful handstand.
And short clowns and tall clowns, both skinny and fat,
    Chase a polka-dot clown with a flower-pot hat.

With so much excitement a circus supplies,
    Three rings are too many for only two eyes.
The merriest moments throughout the whole year
    Are the magical days when the circus is here.

My Favorite Country Memory

Grandma's Butterpress

The house was now old and bore no resemblance to its former grace and dignity. Numerous structural changes and years of misuse and neglect had altered the stately home I remembered. We had moved here to my grandparents' house when I was a young girl, and Papa had made some changes; but no trace seemed to remain of the home I had left at seventeen. It was quiet and lonely as I walked through the empty rooms, trying to recapture the memories of that once lovely old house.

As I climbed the stairs my eyes fell on a familiar shape, long forgotten, lying in a small pile of trash. Could it be? Yes, I remembered the pineapple design! It was Grandma's butterpress!

As I picked it up, my mind rushed back to years ago, in the kitchen of the same old house, where a little girl watched as her grandmother churned butter in a wooden churn. Grandma plunged the long wooden dasher up and down in the soured milk. She let me take a turn too, but my little arm quickly tired. When she lifted the top and removed the dasher, golden butter had formed miraculously—or so it seemed to me—on top of the milk. Who knew that it was in the milk all the time, just needing some coaxing to come alive?

She scooped up the butter, patted it to get out the drops of milk, shaped it into a loose ball, and then placed it in the butterpress. When the butter had cooled, she turned it out onto a dish to reveal the pineapple impression left by the butterpress. It was that same butterpress that I found in a corner of the stairway landing, where it had been forgotten years ago. What a wonderful treasure!

Mary K. Sullivan
Boynton Beach, Florida

The Fourth of July

The Fourth of July was the focal point of summer to me when I was a child. Early on the fourth I was up at the crack of dawn. Even at that early hour, I could hear the firecrackers popping all over our neighborhood. My dad helped me to set off some of our bright red firecrackers, and then he broke them in two and produced what he called cat and dog fights. He had as much fun as I did! The only fireworks deemed safe enough for me to light by myself were the small brown triangles that when touched off by a punk stick would produce black, snakelike spirals. I can't imagine now why I thought those were fun, but I did!

It was hard to wait until dusk; but the time for Dad to set off the nighttime fireworks finally arrived. First he lit the rockets and twirled them up into the air, where they exploded into beautiful, colored fountains. Then he nailed some pinwheels to one of our trees; after they were lit, they whirled around and around with sparks flying. My favorites were the silver mines—silver, triangular pieces that when set off swished up in the air with a bright light. The spectacular display always ended with sparklers, which I loved to swirl in the air to write my name with the glittery light.

Finally, it all came to an end as all days do, and I was encouraged to trudge to bed. Sleepily I did so, with sparkling pictures of the Fourth of July still whirling in my head.

Kathryn Libby
South Portland, Maine

The Day the Circus Came By

One day in 1915 when I was three years old, we had a great surprise. The Ringling Brothers Circus came by *our house!* Usually only an occasional buggy or someone on horseback passed by our home in Arcadia, Louisiana, so the circus procession was quite an event for us. As poor as it was, this road was the main road to Shreveport, and that's where the circus was headed for a performance.

When we saw it all coming, my whole family ran outside and stood under the big oak tree to watch. What a procession passed by! Teams of beautiful horses pulled a long line of circus wagons. Monkeys, lions, tigers, and smaller animals peered out from their cages. The larger animals, such as the giraffes and elephants, walked alongside their keepers. Imagine seeing all those animals walk by our house, animals I had only seen in picture books!

Many wagons contained tents and equipment, and a lot of the circus people were walking to lighten the load on the wagons. At a low spot where water seeped out of the hill, each wagon deepened the ruts until eventually one got stuck. One of the elephant trainers guided an elephant to the rear of the wagon that was mired in the mud. When the trainer gave the order, the elephant put its head against the wagon and pushed it out of the mud hole! The trainer then led the elephant back to its place in the parade, and the great procession continued until it had disappeared down the road.

We felt as if we had gone to the circus right at home! This was truly a red-letter day which we talked about for years to come: "the day the circus came by"!

J. C. Crawford
Monroe, Louisiana

The Ice House

The small crescents from our refrigerator's ice-maker float, symmetrically perfect, in my glass of tea, but they just don't seem as wonderful as those unique chunks of ice we used years ago. Each piece differed in size and shape, depending on how it was knocked off the big block from the ice house; the pieces would crack loudly as we poured the fresh, warm tea over them.

Sometimes on our grocery excursions into town during the hot Texas summertime, Dad and Mom would stop by the ice house after we left the grocery store. While Mom chose some fruits and vegetables at the nearby farmer's market, Dad would pull on over to the ice house, from which the ice man would emerge, carrying his big metal tongs. "How much for you today, neighbor? Fifty cents?"

"Just a quarter block will do me today," Dad would reply. When we made homemade ice cream, he would spring for the fifty-cent size.

Dad would spread out the old quilt in the back of the car, and the ice man would toss the block of ice onto it. "Much obliged," Dad would say as he paid the man and wrapped the quilt around the ice to slow the melting. It was a special treat for us kids to crowd together and ride home next to the big block of melting ice. Sometimes I would pull back the quilt and probe the two holes that the sharp tongs had pierced; if I were lucky, a small shard would break off to cool my mouth on the way home.

At home we chipped off pieces with the ice pick to fill our tall glasses. Everything we cooled with it tasted so pure and clean! There was nothing more refreshing than a tall glass of lemonade tinkling with ice-house ice!

Becky Hejduk
De Queen, Arkansas

Editor's Note: Do you have a holiday or seasonal memory that you'd like to share with the Ideals family of readers? Send your typed memory to:

MY FAVORITE MEMORY
C/O EDITORIAL DEPARTMENT
IDEALS MAGAZINE
535 METROPLEX DRIVE, SUITE 250
NASHVILLE, TENNESSEE 37211

I'D PICK MORE
Daisies

Mildred F. Rowe

If I could live my life again,
I'd be a little lazy;
I'd stop this rushing to and fro
And stop to pick more daisies.

Through all the lovely summer months,
Though days be clear or hazy,
No more to fret o'er tasks undone,
I'd stop to pick a daisy.

Not so important what I did,
This fact time now discloses;
While running through life's garden green,
I'd stop to smell the roses.

If I could hold my little ones—
The children in my care—
I'd scold them less and love them more
With so much love to share.

If I could pass this way again,
Though folks might think I'm crazy,
I'd work and worry less; but I'd
Take time to pick a daisy.

The rush of life has passed me by;
Now I have leisure hours.
But time has taken such a toll;
It's late to pick the flowers.

DAISIES AND LUPINES
Plymouth, New Hampshire
William Johnson/Johnson's Photography

Devotions FROM THE Heart

Pamela Kennedy

"Be ye angry, and sin not:
let not the sun go down upon your wrath."

Ephesians 4:26

COOLING OFF

It was a hot summer day and I had dozens of things to get done. Heading out the door, I had a well-organized list of errands and a plan for accomplishing them. Before long, however, it became evident my best-laid plans were no match for the day. A road crew working on the highway slowed my progress. The grocery store was out of my necessities, and I had to visit two other stores to get what I needed. When I stopped for the dry cleaning, it wasn't ready; and the pharmacy had misplaced my prescription. My internal temperature rose with every frustration, and before long I was slamming the car door each time I got out and giving curt replies to salespeople.

By the time I arrived home, I was looking for a fight. The phone rang and I answered it with a "Hello!" that was more of a challenge than an invitation. On the other end, my husband, swept up in his own swirl of circumstances, reported he would be about an hour late for dinner—again. This was very bad timing on his part, and my reply was less than gracious.

Adrenaline pumping, I went through the house like a tornado, plumping pillows until their stuffing showed at the seams and running the vacuum around the carpet as if I had a tiger by the tail. All the while I rehearsed a speech centered primarily on my hard-working virtue and my husband's lack of appreciation.

With the house straightened and dust free, I slowed long enough to realize I was tired and thirsty. Grabbing a handful of ice cubes from the freezer, I tossed them into a glass and splashed cool tea over them. With a sigh I collapsed in the rocker, closing my eyes against the bright sun streaming in the windows.

Sipping the icy tea, I recalled summer evenings when my mother and I would sit out in the backyard under the cherry trees and have long talks. I'd love to be home now, I thought, pouring out my frustration to her. She always helped me keep my perspective, gently guiding me to look at situations in new ways.

As I rocked, pressing the cold glass against my hot cheek, it was as if I could hear her speaking, "Don't let the sun go down on your anger." I remembered how often she said that when I was upset.

Mother has the ability to release her negative emotions before they damage others; she adopted the Biblical injunction to "be angry and sin not." Recalling this, I realized I can't always keep from becoming angry, but I do have a choice about what I do with that anger—to sin or not to sin! Because of my frustration, I was planning to make my husband pay for working late.

Silently, I asked God to forgive my selfish plotting and dissipate my anger with His love. Slowly, like the cool tea quenching my thirst, I sensed His hand of forgiveness sweep across my weary spirit. I released the pent up anger with a deep sigh, welcoming in its place a quiet peace.

I must have dozed off. Startled by the sound of the door, I opened my eyes to see a beautiful sunset. As my tired husband tossed his briefcase on the chair, I heard my mother's words echo in my mind again.

"Hi," my tentative spouse said, testing the emotional waters before entering the room. The opening words of my rehearsed speech flitted through my mind, then disappeared.

I went to him and gave him a welcoming kiss. Laughing at his puzzled expression, I took him by the hand. "Come on," I urged, "sit here in the rocker, and I'll get you some iced tea. You almost missed the most beautiful sunset of the summer!"

Dear Lord, when I am angry and frustrated, help me to give my feelings to You
and end each day in the freedom of Your peace and forgiveness.
AMEN.

THE CRICKET'S SONG

LaVerne P. Larson

When the light of day has faded
    And night shadows creep along,
It is then the tiny crickets
    Break into their evening song.

I have looked for them, although in vain,
    Because I wished to see
All the merry music makers
    Who perform their songs for me.

But it seems they stay well hidden;
    So I guess they're very shy.
Do they not know that I like them
    More and more as time goes by?

For their soothing, pleasant music
    Gently lulls me into sleep
While the moon and stars above
    A faithful midnight vigil keep.

And I drift afar in lovely dreams;
    But then at break of day,
I awake to find the cricket band
    Slipped silently away.

But I do not grieve because I know
    They will return tonight
To sing their light, enchanting song
    And bring my heart delight.

Amidst a
WILDFLOWER
Regime

Lon Myruski

Within the depths of summer's realm
   The winsome wildflowers reign.
Their colors crown the countryside
   As summer so ordains.
White, tatted tufts of Queen Anne's lace,
   Blue wisps of chicory,
And purple spikes of loosestrife lead
   This aristocracy.

Rich meadows rife with goldenrod
   Display their gilded plumes,
Acclaimed by awestruck passers-by
   As proud, majestic blooms.
And there amidst a sovereignty
   Of untamed, floral scenes,
I wander, paying homage to
   This wondrous, wild regime.

Don't hurry, don't worry.
You're only here for a short visit.
So be sure to stop
and smell the FLOWERS.

—Walter C. Hagen

Readers' Forum

Meet Our Ideals Readers and Their Families

The editors at Ideals are looking for well-written, nostalgic reminiscences, especially about life on the farm. If you have a memory of the treasured days of yesteryear on the farm, send your typed manuscript to: Nostalgic Reminiscences, c/o Editorial Department, Ideals magazine, P.O. Box 305300, Nashville, Tennessee 37230.

Nine-year-old Thomas proudly displays the huge bass he caught with his cousins Josh and Caleb in the pond behind their house in Stillwater, Oklahoma. The boys' grandmother, Gloria Day, knows how much the cousins love to visit one another, so she brings Thomas with her from Oklahoma City whenever she visits her daughter Jenny in Stillwater. Gloria and her husband, Richard, have three children and six grandchildren.

Gloria has loved *Ideals* ever since she was a little girl, and she now also collects *Ideals* hard-cover books.

Bianca, age eight, and Yeshara, age four, enjoy the Independence Day celebration in Berrien Springs, Michigan. Donning colorful hats, the sisters pose in front of the Old County Courthouse for their parents, LUIS AND FELICIA ACOSTA.

When he's not too busy with his duties as pastor, Luis plays and composes music on his trumpet. A skilled seamstress, Felicia's arts and crafts include making chocolate confections and clothing for Bianca and Yeshara. The family lives in Hacienda Heights, California.

THANK YOU Gloria Day and Luis and Felicia Acosta for sharing with *Ideals*. We hope to hear from other readers who would like to share photos and stories with the *Ideals* family. Please include a self-addressed, stamped envelope if you would like the photos returned. Keep your original photographs for safekeeping and send duplicate photos along with your name, address, and telephone number to:

READERS' FORUM
IDEALS PUBLICATIONS INC.
P.O. BOX 305300
NASHVILLE, TENNESSEE 37230

ideals®

Publisher, Patricia A. Pingry
Editor, Lisa C. Ragan
Copy Editor, Michelle Prater Burke
Electronic Prepress Manager,
Tina Wells Davenport
Editorial Assistant, Tara E. Lynn
Editorial Intern, Melissa A. Chronister
Contributing Editors,
Lansing Christman, Deana Deck,
Pamela Kennedy, Patrick McRae,
Mary Skarmeas, Nancy Skarmeas

ACKNOWLEDGMENTS

A FATHER'S WISH from *WHEN DAY IS DONE* by Edgar A. Guest, copyright © 1921 by The Reilly & Lee Co. Used by permission of the author's estate. VAGRANT from *MY HEART WAKETH* by Isla Paschal Richardson, copyright © 1947 by Bruce Humphries, Inc. Used by permission of Branden Publishing, Boston. THE WAKING, copyright © 1953 by Theodore Roethke, from *THE COLLECTED POEMS OF THEODORE ROETHKE* by Theodore Roethke. Used by permission of Doubleday, a division of Bantam Doubleday Dell Publishing Group, Inc. Our sincere thanks to the following author whom we were unable to contact: Mary Dixon Thayer for TREASURES.

THE WAKING

Theodore Roethke

I strolled across
An open field;
The sun was out;
Heat was happy.

This way! This way!
The wren's throat shimmered,
Either to other,
The blossoms sang.

The stones sang,
The little ones did,
And flowers jumped
Like small goats.

A ragged fringe
Of daisies waved;
I wasn't alone
In a grove of apples.

Far in the wood
A nestling sighed;
The dew loosened
Its morning smells.

I came where the river
Ran over stones:
My ears knew
An early joy

And all the waters
Of all the streams
Sang in my veins
That summer day.

"Is life so dear, or peace so sweet, as to be purchased at the price of chains and slavery?
Forbid it, Almighty God!-I know not what course others may take; but as for me,

give me liberty, or give me death!"

Patrick Henry
Richmond, Virginia, March 20, 1775

Ideals Celebrates America's Tradition of Liberty in: THE HERITAGE OF AMERICA

I. A Legacy of Independence . . .
Includes the story of The
Declaration of Independence and
Bill of Rights.
II. Heritage of Courage . . . Be
inspired by Emerson's "Concord
Hymn" and by Francis Scott Key's
"The Star Spangled Banner,"
written in the midst of battle.
III. The Struggle for Liberty . . .
Here is President Lincoln at
Gettysburg and Martin Luther
King, Jr.'s "I Have a Dream."
**IV. The Characteristic of
Exploration . . .** Relive the frontier
through Whittier's "The
Emigrants" and more.
V. A Citadel of Confidence . . .
George M. Cohan's patriotic,
upbeat "Over There" and more.

VI. A Tradition of Faith . . .
Thomas Jefferson prayed
"Almighty God . . . Endow with
the spirit of wisdom those to
whom in Thy Name we entrust
the authority of government . . ."
VII. Our Spirit of Energy . . .
Theodore Roosevelt urged ". . . it
is only through strife . . . that we
shall ultimately win the goal of
true national greatness."
VIII. The Genius of Ingenuity
. . . Without the genius of Thomas
Alva Edison, we would still be in
the dark . . . two Wright brothers,
who owned a bicycle shop, taught
us how to fly . . . and that of
Alexander Graham Bell revolution-
ized how we communicate.

IX. The Right of Creativity . . .
From the poetry of Puritan Anne
Bradstreet to Frank Lloyd Wright's
Guggenheim Museum, our cre-
ativity has thrived.
**X. The Commonality of
Optimism . . .** Roosevelt said,
"The only thing we have to fear is
fear itself" . . . John F. Kennedy
proclaimed the goal "of landing a
man on the moon and returning
him safely to earth."
XI. An Inheritance of Empathy
. . . We empathize with Chief
Seattle, "There was a time when
our people covered the land as the
waves of a wind-ruffled sea cover
its shell paved floor" and by
Emma Lazarus, "Give me your
tired, your poor . . ."

XII. The Spirit of Industriousness
. . . Read about Henry Ford building his first auto in a brick shed in
Detroit and about Henry Kaiser,
whose shipbuilders built and
launched a 10,500-ton ship in 4
days.
XIII. The Quest for Unity . . .
There is no greater speech on
mercy and unity than from
President Lincoln at his second
inaugural address: "With malice
toward none, with charity for all,
with firmness in the right as God
gives us to see the right, let us
strive on to finish the work we are
in, to bind up the nation's wounds
. . . to do all which may achieve a
just and lasting peace among our-
selves and with all nations."

A book with the contents of
THE HERITAGE OF AMERICA
demands exquisite paper, superb
printing, and attention to details of
quality that make it a proud example
of the bookbinder's art. This
magnificent volume is one that truly
deserves a very special place on your
bookshelf . . .

**USE THE ORDER FORM
ON THE REVERSE SIDE
TO ORDER YOUR COPY
TODAY FOR**

30 DAYS FREE!